Who Was
Ponce de León?

by Pam Pollack and Meg Belviso

illustrated by Dede Putra

Penguin Workshop

For Sasha Ponce, Savannah Ponce,
and Elijah Ponce, diverse descendants—PP

For Mason Allen Campanella,
intrepid explorer—MB

PENGUIN WORKSHOP
An imprint of Penguin Random House LLC, New York

First published in the United States of America by Penguin Workshop,
an imprint of Penguin Random House LLC, New York, 2022

Text copyright © 2022 by Pam Pollack and Meg Belviso
Illustrations copyright © 2022 by Penguin Random House LLC

Visit us online at penguinrandomhouse.com.

Library of Congress Cataloging-in-Publication Data is available.

Printed in the United States of America

ISBN 9780399544330 (paperback)   10 9 8 7 6 5 4 3 2 1 WOR
ISBN 9780399544354 (library binding)   10 9 8 7 6 5 4 3 2 1 WOR

Contents

Who Was Ponce de León?

Today, the island of Hispaniola in the Caribbean is divided into two separate nations, Haiti and the Dominican Republic. In the early 1500s, the whole island had been invaded and forced to become a colony of Spain. Hispaniola was ruled by a Spanish governor, Nicolás de Ovando. In 1508, Governor Ovando sent one of the Spanish men living on Hispaniola to explore the nearby island of Borinquén, which the Spanish called San Juan Bautista, but today is called Puerto Rico. The man's name was Juan Ponce de León.

The Spanish governor considered the island of Hispaniola and the people there to be the property of his king and queen. The Spaniards had heard that there was gold in Borinquén, and they wanted all the gold they could get. Any they found had to be shared with King Ferdinand II and Queen Isabella I of Spain, but that still left plenty for a *conquistador*—or conqueror—to keep for himself.

In 1509, Juan Ponce de León returned to Hispaniola from Puerto Rico. Governor Ovando was eager to learn what he had seen and done there. Juan reported that he and his team of fifty men had founded a new settlement they called Caparra. The Taino people who already lived in Puerto Rico were no match for Juan's soldiers and their guns.

Governor Ovando was very pleased with Juan's report. The Spanish had already taken over the island of Hispaniola, enslaving the Indigenous people who lived there. Now, he hoped the Spanish could also rule Puerto Rico.

Governor Ovando rewarded thirty-five-year-old Juan by making him the first governor of Puerto Rico. He would pay him a good salary.

He said that Juan could take a large piece of land in Puerto Rico and build a house on it. He could force the native people of the island to help him build it and work the land. The people of Puerto Rico did not have any choice in the matter.

Juan was thrilled with his new title and the riches that came with it: land, power, and gold. These were the reasons that Juan had left his home in Spain and traveled across the Atlantic Ocean to a world he had never seen before.

CHAPTER 1
A Young Page

Juan Ponce de León was born in 1474 in Santervás del Campo, in the Valladolid province of northwest Spain. His father was Count Juan Ponce de León, a nobleman from a well-respected aristocratic family. The Ponce de Leóns were descended from the Visigoth kings of the Roman period in Spain.

The Visigoths

The Visigoths were one of two groups of people called the Goths who probably originated in Scandinavia. In 378, the Visigoths fought a battle in present-day Turkey against the Roman Empire, then a world superpower. They shocked everyone by winning. Many see this battle as the beginning of the end of the Roman Empire.

After defeating Rome, the Visigoths settled across Western Europe, including on the Iberian Peninsula in Spain. The Visigothic Kingdom was the strongest kingdom in Western Europe for over three hundred years, until they were defeated on that peninsula by Muslim forces in 711.

We don't know who Juan's mother was, because his parents weren't married. That wasn't unusual for the Spanish nobles at that time.

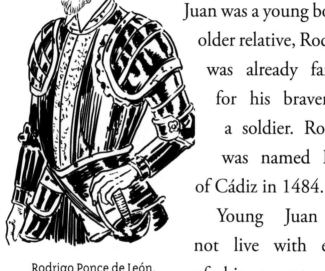

Juan's father was said to have had twenty children from different mothers. By the time Juan was a young boy, an older relative, Rodrigo, was already famous for his bravery as a soldier. Rodrigo was named Duke of Cádiz in 1484.

Young Juan did not live with either of his parents. Like many children of noble families, he was sent to live with a relative at a young age. Juan's guardian was named Pedro Nuñez de Guzman. He had the title of Knight

Rodrigo Ponce de León, the Duke of Cádiz

Commander of the Order of Calatrava and was a personal friend of King Ferdinand. Pedro would teach Juan all the things he needed to know to grow up to be a knight like his famous relative, Rodrigo.

Pedro Nuñez de Guzman

As a boy of noble blood, Juan did not go to school. He was taught by private tutors. Most children in Spain at that time didn't read at all. Juan had access to Pedro's private library, however, and he learned to read and write. He also learned how to behave at court with the king and

queen. As a knight, he would one day serve the throne of Spain. He might very well meet the king and queen in person.

Knights

A knight was a man born to a noble family who was trained to become an honored soldier. Knights served (worked for) either a lord (a person who owned a lot of land) or the king of an entire country. They were known for the metal suits, called armor, that they wore into battle. Even their horses sometimes wore complex suits of armor. If successful, they were given land of their own, and often a title, in exchange for their service.

The word *knight* is also the title granted by a king or queen to one of their subjects to honor them. If a monarch makes a man a knight, he is referred to as "Sir." If a woman is knighted, she is called "Dame."

Spain was a Catholic country, and Juan learned the teachings of his church. He believed that anyone who wasn't Catholic must be converted to Catholicism in order to go to heaven.

Juan's education also focused on horseback riding and hunting. He learned to train hounds to chase animals like deer, boar, and even bears. He also trained birds of prey, including falcons and hawks, to fly away and then return to perch on his arm.

Juan practiced with all the weapons a knight of that time used. That meant learning to fight with a sword and hold a lance while riding on horseback. He also practiced shooting the arquebus, a gun that looked like a long rifle.

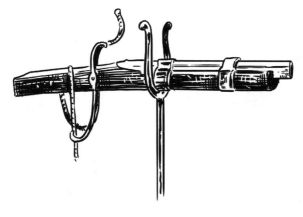

Arquebus

When Juan was still a boy, he began working as a page for his guardian, Pedro. A page was a young man who trained to be a knight by serving one. Juan knew that as a knight he would have to fight and maybe even die to defend the kingdom of Spain. He was ready to do that.

In fact, he couldn't wait to become a real knight. He longed for adventure, to see the world and win glory on the battlefield, as Rodrigo had.

And soon, he would get his chance.

CHAPTER 2
The Battle of Granada

Juan was fourteen years old in 1488. He was ready to go to war and be the soldier that he'd trained to be his whole life.

For hundreds of years, the Catholic leaders of Spain wanted Spain to have only one religion—theirs. In the early eighth century, the Moors, who were Muslim, had invaded from North Africa and won control of the Iberian Peninsula in southwestern Spain. The Catholic Spaniards did  not like any area being under the control of the Moors. The fighting between the two sides went on for centuries.

By 1488, when Juan was ready to join the fight, only one area remained under the control of the Moors: the emirate of Granada. The rulers of Spain, King Ferdinand and Queen Isabella, were united in wanting to drive the Moors out of this region. They gathered troops and weapons to overwhelm the Moors at Granada.

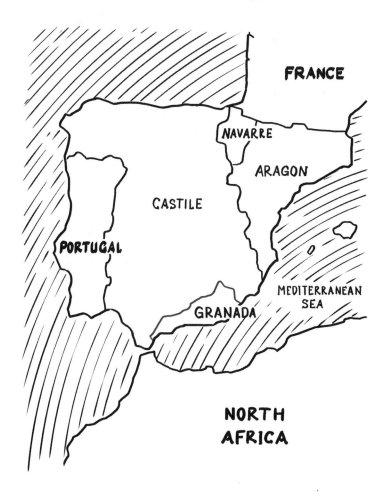

Ferdinand II of Aragon (1452–1516) and Isabella I of Castile (1451–1504)

Before the marriage of Ferdinand and Isabella, the country we call Spain was made up of several small kingdoms. The most powerful were Aragon and Castile. Ferdinand was the king of

Aragon, Isabella the queen of Castile. When they married in 1469, Spain became a united country. The king and queen wanted it to be a Catholic one. They were determined to drive out the Moors, who controlled the smaller kingdom of Granada. So they sponsored voyages to establish trade routes and conquer lands outside their own European kingdom.

Ferdinand and Isabella were second cousins from the same line of royalty. They eventually had five children who all married the heirs of other European royal families.

Rodrigo Ponce de León

The emirate of Granada—the Moorish region—was able to hold out against the Spanish for so long because it was in the mountains and surrounded by towns and forts. Juan's relative Rodrigo was already fighting against the Moors there. He was a war hero whom Queen Isabella described as the "mirror of chivalry."

When Juan joined the Spanish soldiers fighting their way toward Granada, it was ruled by the young sultan Abu Abdallah Muhammad XII. His forces weren't strong enough to fight against modern weapons like cannons and bombards, which fired heavy granite balls from far away. That meant the Spanish soldiers didn't have to

Abu Abdallah Muhammad XII

move in close to fight as they had in the past. They could also rely on their long arquebus rifles. Unlike earlier guns, these could be fired by a single man.

To complicate matters, the Moors were used to fighting only in mild weather. When winter set in, soldiers and commanders returned home.

But under Ferdinand and Isabella, the Spanish soldiers were paid year-round and equipped for colder weather. That meant Juan fought year-round—and he fought so bravely that he came to the attention of the king and queen.

Juan and the other soldiers reached Granada in April 1491. They surrounded the city so that no one could get in or out or get food inside. Muhammad XII hoped to receive help from Egypt and Morocco, in northern Africa, but no help came. After eight months, the sultan surrendered Granada to Ferdinand and Isabella. He opened the doors of his city to them, saying, "These are the keys of this paradise."

Islam

Islam, the Muslim faith, is the world's second largest religion, practiced by 1.8 billion people around the world. Muslims believe that Allah (God) spoke to the prophet Muhammad through the angel Gabriel. God's words were then written down in a holy book called the Quran. The central belief of Islam is that "There is no god but Allah and Muhammad is his messenger."

Muhammad was born in 570 in the city of Mecca, which Muslims now call their holy city. It is located in the Sirat Mountains of Saudi Arabia.

The Holy City of Mecca

Muslims and Jews would later be given this choice: either convert to Christianity or leave Spain. Victory at Granada convinced the Spanish king and queen that they were superior to their enemies and that God wanted them to win.

Spain was now a completely Catholic country. Because of their victory over the Moors, they believed they should go out and search for other lands to conquer and to spread their Catholic faith.

They would need conquistadors—from the Spanish word for *conqueror*—to explore new lands for them. These knights and soldiers would sail forth from Europe, opening trade routes and claiming land for their home countries. Ferdinand and Isabella thought Juan, now eighteen years old, was just the kind of conquistador they needed.

CHAPTER 3
Conquest

Juan had spent his whole life training to be a soldier, and maybe one day even a knight.

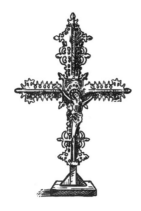

Now that the war in Granada was over, what would he do next? Ferdinand and Isabella were eager to follow through on what they believed was their assignment from God: to conquer other lands, to establish new colonies, and to spread the Catholic faith.

In 1492, an explorer named Christopher Columbus had landed on the island Hispaniola in the Caribbean Sea and seized it as a colony for Spain. Juan already knew Columbus. They had both been present at the surrender of Granada. Juan learned that Columbus was planning to return to Hispaniola to build Spanish settlements there. Spanish colonists would establish farms and mine for gold. They would make money for the Spanish king and queen. Hispaniola was already populated by people called the Taino. They did not want their island to be conquered and become a part of the kingdom of Spain, and they certainly didn't want to work for the Spanish.

Christopher Columbus

Colonization

Colonization is when one powerful country claims control of another, often less powerful—or uninhabited—country or region. A long-established nation like England or Spain could easily overpower smaller areas populated by Indigenous people, settle in, and take control of the region. They then took natural resources like minerals (including gold and silver), crops,

Gold items belonging to people in Central and South America were melted down and formed into small gold bars that were then sent to Spain.

and timber to export back to their own country. The controlling country grows wealthy, the smaller country is looted. The native people are oppressed.

Many places that are no longer officially colonies still suffer from the effects of colonization. Many treasures, like artwork, architecture, and religious items made by native people, still remain in the museums of former colonial powers, where they were sent long ago.

So when Columbus returned to Hispaniola, he planned to bring soldiers to force the Taino to do what he wanted.

Columbus left Spain to return to Hispaniola on September 25, 1493, with seventeen ships and

about 1,300 men. One of those men was nineteen-year-old Juan Ponce de León. Juan wasn't solely interested in conquering new lands for Spain. As a conquistador, he would be able to keep some of the profits he found in Hispaniola for himself.

When Columbus had returned to Spain after his first voyage, he left behind a large group of Spanish soldiers. Juan and the other men on the 1493 voyage expected to be greeted by them when they arrived on the island. But when they reached

Hispaniola, they found that all the Spaniards were dead. Some had died from disease, and others had been killed by the Taino, who were trying to defend themselves and their home. Columbus was ready to defeat the Taino.

The Taino

The Taino were one of the many groups that made up the Arawakan Indians of northeastern South America. They lived on the group of islands known as the Greater Antilles: Cuba, Jamaica, Hispaniola (Haiti and the Dominican Republic), and Puerto Rico. The Taino probably first started settling these areas between AD 120 and 400. Before the arrival of Europeans, some historians believe there may have been as many as eight million Taino. They were sailors, fishermen, canoe makers, and navigators. They lived in thatch houses, and wore earrings, nose rings, and necklaces.

The Taino had a rich religious tradition that they passed down through ceremonial dances called *areytos*, drumbeats, oral traditions, and a ceremonial ball game played on fields marked by stones called *dolmens*.

In the Taino culture, both men and women could be chiefs.

As a Spanish soldier, Juan was ready to force the Taino of Hispaniola to work for Spain, and he had modern weapons that the Taino didn't. It was not an equal fight. He and his fellow soldiers killed many and enslaved many others until the Taino admitted defeat. With the Spaniards now in control of the island, Columbus prepared to return to Spain. Juan chose to stay behind and make his home on Hispaniola. He met a Spanish woman named Leonora, whose father was an innkeeper there. The two were married around 1502. When Columbus sailed back to Spain, Nicolás de Ovando was appointed governor of Hispaniola.

Nicolás de Ovando

In 1504, the Taino people attacked the Spanish settlement in Higüey (say: ee-GWAY), on the eastern side of the island. Ovando ordered Juan to lead four hundred Spanish soldiers against them. The Taino outnumbered Juan and his men four to one, and yet they were crushed.

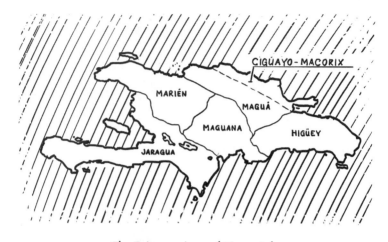

The Taino regions of Hispaniola

Ovando rewarded Juan by appointing him frontier governor in charge of the entire province where Higüey was located. Juan also received a large piece of land and a group of enslaved Taino who were forced to work for him.

CHAPTER 4
Frontier Governor

Frontier Governor Juan had never owned land of his own before. He had always been a soldier who moved with the army. Now he had a chance to build wealth for himself. Once the Taino were defeated, the Spanish officially took over the whole island of Hispaniola and divided it up among themselves. Juan set to work to learn how to raise horses, pigs, and cattle.

He also wanted to grow crops. Unlike other conquistadors, Juan knew the Taino had things to teach him. Since this had been their land for hundreds of years, they knew how to raise native crops like sweet potatoes and a root vegetable called cassava.

It didn't bother Juan that he was asking the Taino to help him raise crops on land that he had helped take from them by force. He believed that

Spain had every right to conquer this country for itself. It didn't matter to him that the Taino people were already living there and considered it their home. He didn't see them as equals to himself or any Spaniard.

Back in Spain, Juan would not have been able to enslave another white Spanish person, no matter how poor they were. But he may have been taught that God had created some people to be superior to others. And as a Catholic and a Spaniard, he felt he was superior to the Taino.

Juan's land was on the eastern side of Hispaniola. There he built a big stone house for himself and Leonora. They started a family and soon had two children: a son, Luis, and a daughter, Juana. In 1505, Governor Ovando gave Juan permission to establish a new town in Higüey, which he called Salvaleón.

Juan served as frontier governor in Higüey for about three years. During that time, he sometimes met and traded with free Taino from a neighboring island. Juan still thought he had things to learn from the Taino. He was especially interested when they described the rich lands of the island they called Borinquén.

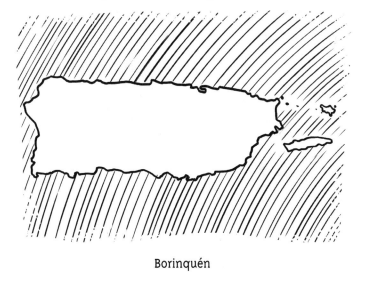

Borinquén

Even though Juan was already very comfortable and wealthy in Hispaniola, he still wanted more. So did King Ferdinand. Perhaps Juan also missed traveling to fight in wars and sailing to unknown lands. He had been raised to be a soldier. Life on a plantation, even a prosperous one, was not exciting enough for him.

Juan was looking for his next challenge, and Borinquén would be it.

CHAPTER 5
Borinquén

Juan couldn't wait to explore Borinquén. In 1508, after he received permission from Governor Ovando and King Ferdinand, he gathered together forty soldiers and a single ship. He landed 230 miles away on the west side of the island and made a settlement in a spot about 10 miles away from what is now the city of San Juan. Juan, as always, was ready to fight any native people who tried to interfere with his crew. But the leader of the Taino on Borinquén, the cacique (say: ku-SEEK) called Aguay, had heard about the terrible weapons of the Spanish. (The cacique is a native chief.) He decided it would be better for the Taino of Borinquén to give up without a fight.

Juan set up a farming colony called Caparra where he continued raising pigs and cattle, as well as native crops like cassava and sweet potatoes.

Cassava was an especially valuable crop because it could be used to make bread that did not rot in sea air. That meant Juan could sell the bread to ships planning to cross the Atlantic Ocean and return to Spain. The sailors would have good bread to eat on the long journey.

Cassava

Governor Ovando was so pleased with the new colony that he appointed Juan governor of Borinquén. (The Spanish would later decide the island needed a new name—a Spanish one. So in 1521 they changed the name to *Puerto Rico*, which means "rich port.") Juan brought his family from Hispaniola to settle with him in Puerto Rico. There he and Leonora had two more daughters, Maria and Isabel. Juan also had a pet dog—a Spanish mastiff with red fur called Becerillo. It was said he could distinguish a friend from an enemy by smell and was a fierce fighter.

Juan said he was "the equal of fifty men" in battle. Becerillo was well-known on the island.

It was Juan's job to make his new island home a success for Spain. It was, after all, a colony now owned by the king. He enslaved the Taino to work for the colonists on Spanish plantations instead of their own land. So eventually, they had no food for themselves. Sometimes the Spanish even forced mothers to work, separating them from their infants, who could die without them.

The newcomers hurt the Taino further by infecting them with European diseases. When Spanish settlers arrived in Hispaniola and Puerto Rico, they brought diseases that the native people had never encountered, like smallpox, measles, and influenza. The native people had no immunity—no natural defenses—to these diseases and no medicine to fight them. The Spanish colonists killed off entire native villages just by their presence on the island.

The Taino were not the only group of native people on the island of Puerto Rico at that time. A people called the Caribs lived on the other side of the island. The Caribs were fierce warriors who sometimes captured and enslaved the Taino. When the Spanish soldiers took over Taino territory, they promised they would protect them from the Caribs on the eastern side of the island, but they broke that promise. The Spaniards let the Carib raids continue against the Taino.

Eventually the Taino could take no more of this treatment. In 1511, just three years after Juan Ponce de León arrived, they rebelled against the Spanish. Juan ordered his men to launch a surprise nighttime attack. They killed thousands of the

Taino, who were already weakened by hunger, exhaustion, and disease.

Ferdinand considered Juan to be very good at his job.

Diego Columbus

Juan's success in Puerto Rico drew the attention of a lot of people from Spain. One of them had a very personal interest in the island. Diego Columbus was the son of Christopher Columbus. In 1509, he had arrived in Hispaniola with his family. Diego was already rich and had the title of Governor of the Indies. (The Indies were what the Spanish called the area that included the islands of the Caribbean Sea.) Diego's father had stopped briefly on the island of Puerto Rico in 1493, just long enough to claim it for Spain. Therefore, Diego claimed, he was the rightful governor of Puerto Rico, not Juan.

Diego Columbus went to King Ferdinand with his claim. In 1511, the royal court decided that "by right of his father's discovery" Diego was the true governor of Puerto Rico.

The West Indies

When Christopher Columbus set out from Spain, he sailed west hoping to find what he called the Indies, which included modern nations like China and India. Columbus did not reach Asia, but he found a group of islands in the Caribbean Sea that he mistook for his destination. Therefore, he called them the Indies. When people realized that he had made a mistake, they began calling the newly discovered region the West Indies. The West Indies encompasses the triangle from Florida south along the coast of Central America, eastward along the coast of South America, and northward to Bermuda. The region is also called the Caribbean Basin.

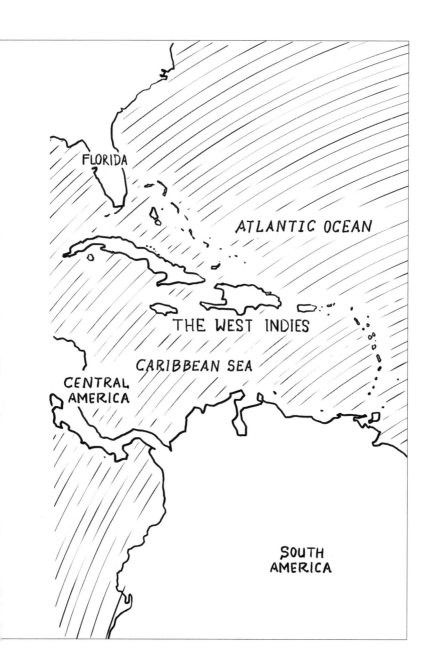

FLORIDA

ATLANTIC OCEAN

THE WEST INDIES

CARIBBEAN SEA

CENTRAL
AMERICA

SOUTH
AMERICA

Juan lost his position. But Diego was still jealous of the way people respected Juan.

Although he loved Puerto Rico, Juan needed to move on. Once again, he listened to the native people of Puerto Rico. They often talked about a land to the north which they sometimes called Bimini. Juan decided to find it for himself.

He got permission from King Ferdinand

to sail north in 1512. Even though Juan hadn't yet found this new land—and didn't even know if it really existed—he was given the title Adelantado of Bimini (another type of governor) and was told he could keep one-tenth of anything he found there. He was also named governor for life of Bimini and any other new land he encountered.

Juan was given a statement to read to the people he found living in any of the regions he landed in. The statement, called the Spanish Requerimiento of 1513, said that God wanted Spain to rule the whole world. If the people

in these lands refused to immediately become Catholic and submit, Spain would do to them "all the mischief and damage" that it could. That meant killing them, enslaving them, and stealing everything from them.

Because he wasn't a soldier, Diego did not know how to defeat the Caribs. They even burned down the governor's house, and Juan's wife and children were almost killed. In 1512, Juan led an attack on the Caribs that drove them back from the Spanish settlement.

Juan hired three ships and a crew with his own

money. He would feed them with food from his own plantation back in Hispaniola. Juan himself was not a sailor. He didn't know how to steer a ship in the right direction. He couldn't tell where he was on the open sea. For that he depended on the navigator Antón de Alaminos. In Juan's time, navigators had to rely either on the positions of the stars to guide their way, or on dead reckoning. Using direction, distance, and speed, dead reckoning could determine a ship's position. It wasn't an easy thing to do, but Alaminos was the best at it.

Antón de Alaminos (c. 1478–?)

Antón de Alaminos was born on the southern coast of Spain. As a young man, he sailed on ships from the Canary Islands down the coast of Africa, and he became an expert at "reading water." That meant he could understand hidden

Antón de Alaminos

currents deep beneath the surface of the water. Antón sailed on Columbus's second voyage across the Atlantic Ocean with Juan Ponce de León. His skills made him the most sought-after navigator of his time. Anyone sailing the Caribbean Sea in the fifteenth century wanted Antón de Alaminos to be the navigator.

CHAPTER 7
La Florida

On March 3, 1513, thirty-nine-year-old Juan was ready to sail north. His three ships were the *Santiago*, the *San Cristóbal*, and the *Santa Maria de la Consolación*. He had loaded provisions for the journey, most of which were grown on Juan's own plantation in Hispaniola. He had his beard trimmed close to his jawline by the ship's surgeon. At that time, a ship's surgeon—who had not gone to medical school—could pull a tooth, sew up a cut, or amputate an arm or leg if it became infected. The surgeon was also a barber who cut hair and shaved men's beards.

They sailed for about a month. On April 2, the three ships landed on the coast of what looked to Juan like an island. But it was actually

The *Santiago*

a peninsula, a piece of land surrounded by water on only three sides. It was connected to a whole continent—what is now North America.

Looking around at the new land, he saw bright flowers, birds, and butterflies. He named the land *La Florida*, which means *flowery*. He thought this was an especially good name,

because he had landed there during the Easter season. Easter is the most important Catholic holy day of the year, and the Easter season was called *Pascua Florida*, or the Feast of Flowers, in Spanish.

Juan had landed in a spot that today is thought to be part of Saint Augustine, in the state of Florida. He and his crew camped for five days, then returned to their ships. A few days later, the *Santa Maria* and the *Santiago* landed again and realized they had lost their third ship. The ocean current we now call the Gulf Stream had carried the *San Cristóbal* back out to sea and out of sight. All the men could do was wait for it to come back.

The land they had named *La Florida* was already home to many people. Some of them tried to drive the Spanish away. Juan did not want to leave Florida, but he did move his men in an attempt to avoid the local people.

The Gulf Stream

The sea is always in motion, with currents that move from one place to another. The Gulf Stream is caused by a system of circular currents and winds. They create what is called an oceanic gyre. When warm water from the Gulf of Mexico flows north into the Atlantic Ocean, the colder Atlantic water sinks and moves south. The Gulf Stream is thousands of miles long. It carries warm water from the Gulf of Mexico all the way up to the Norwegian Sea! The colder water flows south all the way to Antarctica.

Some credit Antón de Alaminos as the first navigator to make use of the Gulf Stream. For more than two hundred years after its discovery in 1513, Spanish ships used the Gulf Stream current on their trade routes but never marked it on maps. They wanted to keep it a secret because it helped

the Spanish ships travel faster than other ships.
The first mention of the Gulf Stream on a printed
map was not until 1769.

They camped by a stream that Juan named *Rio de la Cruz* or "River of the Cross." At the stream, Juan and his men gathered as much firewood as they could. They also captured a local man and forced him to act as their guide.

The *San Cristóbal* finally reappeared, and the three ships set sail again, following the shore west before landing once more. This area was inhabited by people called the Calusa, who were known for their fierceness. Their cacique was called Calus. Juan called him Carlos, because that's what the name sounded like to him. From then on, the Spanish mistakenly called all native tribal leaders Carlos.

Juan hoped he could convince the Calusa to let him and his men stay on the land. But Calus of the Calusa had heard all about what the Spaniards did when they arrived in places like Hispaniola and Puerto Rico. He did not want that happening on his land. Discussions

between the Calusa and the Spanish did not go well. Eventually, a battle broke out. The Calusa attacked the Spaniards with arrows made even more deadly with sharpened fish bones.

After the attack by the Calusa, Juan made the decision to leave the mainland. He ordered his men back on the ships and headed south toward home.

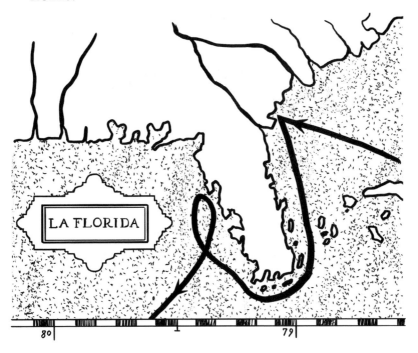

On his way back to Puerto Rico, Juan came across another chain of islands on the west end of what are now called the Florida Keys. The waters around them were filled with animals, including

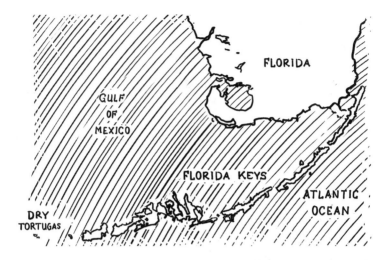

sea turtles. The sailors hunted and caught many
of them and had a big feast. They were thrilled to
have something to eat besides their usual meal of
rice and beans cooked in pig fat.

Juan named the islands Las Tortugas or "The
Turtles." Today the islands are called the Dry
Tortugas because there is no fresh water on them.

CHAPTER 8
A Spanish Hero

When Juan got back to Puerto Rico, he no longer had a house there. Diego Columbus was still governor, and he still didn't like Juan. So Juan decided to take his family back to Spain. He didn't plan to live there, but he wanted to report to King Ferdinand personally about his new discovery, the land he called Florida.

Juan and his family left Puerto Rico in April 1514. King Ferdinand was very happy to see Juan when he arrived at the court in Valladolid in Spain. The king was also pleased to hear about Florida, which Juan still described as an island. Juan also told the king about the land the Taino called Bimini, and that he hoped to find it.

As a reward for reporting back to him about
Florida, the king gave Juan his own coat of arms.
This meant that Juan could design a symbol for
his family to put on his shield. It also meant
that his family was very highly honored. The

king had to give his permission to create a coat of arms. Juan chose to put a lion on his family's coat of arms. He was the first conquistador to receive this honor.

Juan made an important visit to the Casa de Contratación (say: con-tra-ta-SYON) in the city of Seville. This was where the Spanish government kept track of everything that went on in the New World that Juan was helping to conquer. This world wasn't new, of course. It only seemed that way to the Spanish sailors who had never seen it before.

Juan gave the record-keepers there a detailed description of all the lands he had seen. They were then added to the map called the *Padrón Real* or Royal Register. This map was used to make all the official navigation charts used by Spanish sea captains and pilots. To Spain, this map represented the whole world. If a place wasn't on the map, Spanish sea captains didn't know about it.

While in Spain, Juan signed a contract that said he had the right to settle and become governor of both Florida and Bimini. The contract promised that he would be governor for life.

This was important to Juan, because he did not want to have his job taken away from him, as Diego Columbus had done in Puerto Rico.

Although Juan was the governor of these lands in the eyes of Spain, he couldn't really rule either of them yet. Bimini was a land he had only heard people talk about. He still had not located it. He had landed in Florida, but was quickly chased away by the Calusa, who had lived there for thousands of years. They did not consider Juan to be their governor. The Calusa had their own rulers. If Juan was going to govern the Calusa, he would have to fight them like he had the Taino and the Caribs.

Before Juan could return to Florida, King Ferdinand II had another request. The Carib tribe had continued to attack Spanish settlements in and around the Caribbean Basin. The king wanted Juan to organize an armada, a fleet of Spanish warships, to protect those settlements. After he fought the Caribs, he could try to settle Florida and become governor there.

The Calusa

The Calusa were descendants of the Caloosahatchee people who started settling in Florida in AD 500. They built their homes on stilts with roofs made out of woven palmetto leaves and caught shellfish like conchs, crabs, clams, lobsters, and oysters. They used the shells for tools, jewelry, and ornaments for their shrines. They used deerskin, woven palm fronds, and moss to make clothing.

The Calusa lived on the southwest coast of Florida, but they traveled as far away as Cuba in dugout canoes made from hollowed-out cypress logs. The name *Calusa* means "Fierce People."

CHAPTER 9
A New King

Juan left Spain with his armada on May 14, 1515. The Caribs had been attacking Spanish settlements wherever they could find them. The fight was scattered over thousands of miles in the Lesser Antilles, a group of volcanic islands

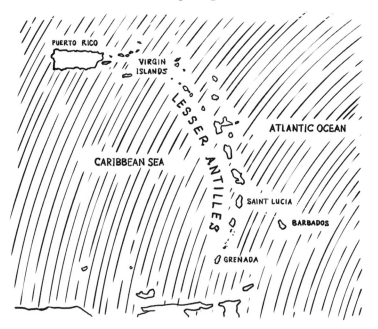

in the Caribbean Sea. Juan fought many battles with the Caribs on many different islands.

On January 23, 1516, King Ferdinand II died. Ferdinand had been Juan's biggest supporter in Spain. Juan worried that with Ferdinand gone, he might lose the many things the king had given him, such as his contract to explore Florida and maybe even his knighthood. Queen Isabella had already died twelve years earlier. Ferdinand's throne—his kingdom—was inherited by his grandson, Charles I,

King Charles I of Spain

who would rule over not only Spain but later also lands in what are today Germany, Austria, and Italy as Holy Roman Emperor Charles V. At this time he was only sixteen years old.

Juan knew it was important for King Charles to like him. He decided to end his battles with the Caribs and sail back to Spain. Juan did have supporters in Spain, including Cardinal Francisco Jiménez de Cisneros. Cardinal Francisco was running the Spanish government while it transitioned from Ferdinand to Charles. Juan was happy for that support, but he did not think he could leave right away. He needed to wait until he was sure King Charles planned to honor the contract Juan had made with his grandfather, Ferdinand II.

While he was in Spain, Juan's wife Leonora died. He met and married his second wife, Juana de Pineda of Seville.

Juan was eager to return to Puerto Rico. He had heard that other Spanish explorers were making trips to "his" Florida. They didn't have Spain's permission to settle Florida, or the title that Juan had been given. But they did share a common enemy: The Calusa warriors who had driven Juan away drove them out, too.

The Calusa knew when the Spanish were coming because other tribes had warned them. These tribes included the Tequesta, the Ais, and the Jeaga on the east coast of Florida, the Guacata in Central Florida, and the Cuchiyaga in the Florida Keys. As the Calusa were the most powerful people in the area, these other tribes brought them gifts and tried to stay on friendly terms with them. Helping the Calusa against the Spanish was a smart way to do that.

The Fountain of Youth

Today, many people think of Juan Ponce de León as the man who searched for—and possibly found—the Fountain of Youth, a magical spring that would make an old person young again. This story is now thought to have been made up by a man named Gonzalo Fernández de Oviedo y Valdés, who was a Spanish historian living in the West Indies. Oviedo was a friend of Diego Columbus. He may have invented the story just to make Juan look foolish.

Even though it wasn't real, the legend captured people's imaginations at the time, and still does today.

There are several springs in Florida that people have claimed to be the "real" Fountain of Youth, and some of them are even named after Juan. In Saint Augustine, Florida, thousands of tourists come to taste the sulfur-smelling waters at the

Fountain of Youth Archaeological Park, believing them to be linked to Juan Ponce de León.

In 1878, *Harper's Monthly* magazine published an article claiming that the Fountain of Youth was actually located in Arkansas, whose hot springs have healing properties.

The Bimini islands in the Bahamas also claim to be the home of Juan's Fountain of Youth: a small freshwater well along the road to the South Bimini Airport.

Even though his other expeditions had failed, Juan wanted to get back to Florida as soon as possible. Everyone in Spain was talking about all the land and treasure another conquistador, Hernán Cortés, had collected for Spain, and that made Juan jealous.

Juan left Spain in 1518 and returned to Puerto Rico. In 1521, he gathered a crew and two ships. On board were farmers with their cattle, sheep, and pigs as well as seeds to plant crops. Juan brought men who knew how to build with wood and metal, and soldiers with horses and dogs. He also brought priests to convert the native people of Florida to the Catholic faith. Also on board was Juan's nephew, Hernán. Juan was ready to make a second expedition to Florida. This time he was determined to conquer it and settle there.

Hernán Cortés (1485–1547)

Hernán Cortés was born to a noble family in Medellin, Spain. He sailed from Spain in 1504 and first landed in Hispaniola. He joined an expedition to Cuba in 1511, eventually becoming the mayor of Santiago there.

He commanded his own expedition to Mexico in 1519. At that time, the Aztecs ruled between five million and six million people in Central Mexico. Cortés joined with some native people who did not want to be ruled by the Aztecs. With their help, he defeated the Aztecs in the Battle of Otumba on July 7, 1520. As a reward, he was appointed governor, captain general, and chief justice of the entire region, called New Spain, in 1522.

Cortés eventually returned to Seville, Spain, where he died at age sixty-two.

CHAPTER 10
The Calusa

In February 1521, Juan left Puerto Rico to return to Florida. He is believed to have landed on what is today Sanibel Island, off the coast of Southwest Florida. This spot had everything a man looking to start a colony wanted: deep water that made a good port for ships, good drinking water, and a position Juan could defend from attack.

Juan learned that Sanibel Island was right across the bay from where Calus, cacique of the Calusa, lived (now Estero Island). It is on the southeast side of what is today called San Carlos Bay.

Calus and his warriors quickly attacked. The Spanish men chased them off the island with their guns.

Juan hoped the Calusa would now leave the settlers alone. But the Calusa fought against the Spanish invaders. They attacked when the settlers were trying to plant their crops, feed their animals, and build shelter. It seemed that anytime they were out in the open and unprotected, the settlers were targets for the Calusa.

Even though the Spanish settlers had better weapons, they were vastly outnumbered by the relentless Calusa. Juan and his crew finally decided they had to leave—and they had to move out quickly. They didn't even have time to load their horses back onto the ships.

They had to fight the Calusa even as they tried to return to their boats. In the fight, Juan was hit in the thigh by a Calusa warrior's reed arrow. He made it onto the ship with the help of his men, and they set sail for nearby Cuba to get medical help. Juan's nephew Hernán was also wounded. He died before they reached Cuba.

Juan made it to Cuba, but the arrow wound was already infected and making him sick. In July 1521, less than a year after he set out to conquer Florida and become its governor, Juan died. He was forty-seven years old. He was buried in Cuba, but later his body was moved to San Juan, Puerto Rico. Today his body lies in the Cathedral of San Juan under a monument that reads: "Beneath this structure rest the bones of a Lion."

Tomb of Ponce de León

Juan Ponce de León's home that was turned into a museum

Today, the land where Juan built his house is in the country of the Dominican Republic. The house itself is now a museum in the city of San Rafael de Yuma. There are islands in the Bahamas called Bimini. The name means "two islands" in the language of the Lucayan people who lived there. Could it be the mystical land Juan hoped to find? We'll never know.

Although he never ruled Florida or found Bimini, Juan Ponce de León and men like him completely changed the lands they conquered. After Juan's death, the Spanish continued to invade other lands in order to create what they called a New Spain. Everywhere they colonized, they took natural resources like minerals and crops for themselves. The people who lived there were enslaved and forced to work for Spain. The Spanish later brought more enslaved people from Africa as well. Today many people who live in areas like Cuba and Puerto Rico are descended from the Spanish conquerors, native people, and enslaved Africans.

For many years, men like Juan were celebrated for their bravery in exploring "new" worlds. Statues were created to honor them. But they were mapping places they had never been to before, not discovering them. In his lifetime, Juan was considered a hero by the people in Spain.

Today, people question whether someone should be praised for "discovering" a land that they actually took by force from the people who lived there.

In the time of Ponce de León, men dreamed of sailing away to claim land and treasure. Like the myth of the Fountain of Youth, those dreams weren't based in a shared reality. They brought glory and riches to Spain, but to the people whose lands Juan helped conquer, they brought sadness, pain, and the end of the life they loved.

Juan Ponce de León lived the very life he longed for when he was growing up. He was a knight who earned the honor and respect of his king and queen. He saw lands that he didn't even know existed when he was a boy. He was hailed as a hero by the people of his country and believed he was doing holy work for his God. He may have been only forty-seven when he died, but hundreds of years later, he is still remembered. The name Juan Ponce de León is forever connected to the histories of Florida, Puerto Rico, and Bimini.

Monument to Juan Ponce de León in San Juan, Puerto Rico

Timeline of Ponce de León's Life

1474 — Juan Ponce de León is born in Santervás del Campo, Spain

1492 — Fights in the final battle for Granada, making Spain an entirely Catholic country

1493 — Sails to Hispaniola with Christopher Columbus

c. 1502 — Marries Leonora

1504 — Appointed frontier governor of Higüey on Hispaniola

1505 — Founds the town of Salvaleón in Higüey on Hispaniola

1508 — Leads expedition to the island of Borinquén (later named Puerto Rico)

1509 — Becomes governor of Puerto Rico

1511 — Crushes Taino rebellion in Puerto Rico

1512 — Receives permission from King Ferdinand II of Spain to explore lands north of Puerto Rico

1513 — Lands on the coast of Florida for the first time

1514 — Named governor for life of Florida and Bimini by King Ferdinand II of Spain

1516 — Returns to Spain after the death of King Ferdinand II

1518 — Leaves Spain to return to the Caribbean

1521 — Returns to Florida and is injured by the Calusa

— Dies from arrow injury in Cuba in July

Timeline of the World

1475 — First recorded game of chess is played with modern rules, between Francesco di Castellvi and Narciso Vinyoles in Spain

1476 — Vlad III, Prince of Wallachia, known as Vlad the Impaler or Vlad Dracula, dies north of modern-day Bucharest, Romania

c. 1481 — The Aztec Calendar Stone or Sun Stone is carved

1483 — Martin Luther, founder of Protestantism, is born in Germany

1487 — The *Malleus Maleficarum*, a manual for witch-hunters, is published in Speyer, Germany

1490 — Leonardo da Vinci designs an oil lamp with a flame inside a glass tube inside a glass globe filled with water

1502 — The first enslaved Africans are forcibly brought to the island of Hispaniola

1506 — Pope Julius II lays the foundation stone of the current-day St. Peter's Basilica in Rome

1508 — Michelangelo begins painting the Sistine Chapel ceiling in the Vatican in Rome

1516 — Henry VIII establishes the British postal service

1520 — Ferdinand Magellan becomes the first European to sail from the Atlantic Ocean to the Pacific

Bibliography

*Books for young readers

Cusick, James G., and Sherry Johnson (editors). *The Voyages of Ponce de León: Scholarly Perspectives*. Cocoa, FL: Florida Historical Society Press, 2012.

*Eagen, Rachel. *Ponce de León: Exploring Florida and Puerto Rico*. In the Footsteps of Explorers series. New York: Crabtree Publishing, 2006.

Evanoff, Neely. "Pirates and the Gulf Stream and World Conquest." *Medium*. May 28, 2018. https://medium.com/@ngevanoff/the-gulf-stream-was-discovered-in-a-high-speed-chase-7c8e4ccfb720.

Florida Center for Instructional Technology. "The Calusa: The 'Shell Indians.'" *Exploring Florida*. https://fcit.usf.edu/florida/lessons/calusa/calusa1.htm.

National Oceanic and Atmospheric Administration. "What Is the Gulf Stream?" *Scijinks*. May 11, 2021. https://scijinks.gov/gulf-stream/.

Peck, Douglas T. *Ponce de León and the Discovery of Florida: The Man, the Myth, and the Truth*. St. Paul, MN: Pogo Press, 1993.

Rivera, Magaly. "Taino Indian Culture.": *Welcome to Puerto Rico!* https://welcome.topuertorico.org/reference/taino.shtml.

*Sammons, Sandra Wallus. *Juan Ponce de León and the Discovery of Florida*. Sarasota, FL: Pineapple Press, 2013.

Stoneking, Cain. "The Decline of the Tainos, 1492–1542: A Re-Vision." *Student Theses, Papers and Projects (History)*. 2009. https://digitalcommons.wou.edu/cgi/viewcontent.cgi?article=1222&context=his#:~:text=Early%20population%20estimates%20of%20the,from%20100%2C000%20to%201%2C000%2C000%20people.

*Waxman, Laura Hamilton. *A Journey with Ponce de León*. Primary Source Explorers series. Minneapolis: Lerner Publications, 2018.

YOUR HEADQUARTERS FOR HISTORY

Activities, Mad Libs, and sidesplitting jokes!
Discover the Who HQ books beyond the biographies